I LOVE MEN

I LOVE MEN

MARÍA ORTÍZ

Library of Congress Control Number:		2016913958
ISBN:	Hardcover	978-1-5065-1607-3
	Softcover	978-1-5065-1606-6
	eBook	978-1-5065-1608-0

Print information available on the last page.

Rev. date: 31/08/2016

To order additional copies of this book, contact:
Palibrio
1663 Liberty Drive
Suite 200
Bloomington, IN 47403
Toll Free from the U.S.A 877.407.5847
Toll Free from Mexico 01.800.288.2243
Toll Free from Spain 900.866.949
From other International locations +1.812.671.9757
Fax: 01.812.355.1576
orders@palibrio.com
744139

CONTENTS

FROM BABIES TO ELDERS 1

FAMILY ROLE 29

THE PROFESSIONAL MAN.........................39

WITH ADJECTIVES 61

THE ARTISTS.................................79

THE FUNNY THING 95

THE UNFORGETTABLE...........................107

THIS IS THE ENGLISH VERSION OF "ME ENCANTAN LOS HOMBRES" WHICH WAS MADE IN SPANISH AND RELEASED ON MAY, 2016.

WE ARE A TEAM OF PEOPLE AT WORK MAKING THIS PROJECT BECOMES A REALITY... IF YOU FIND YOUR SELF HAVING A HARD TIME UNDERSTANDING THE MEANING, JUST LET YOUR SOUL GUIDE YOU TROUGH THE END. SHE HAS A HIGHER UNDERSTANDING THAT IS GIVING AND LOVING AND DOES NOT JUDGE OR CONDEMN.

THIS IS A SHORT BOOK BUT, IT HAS BEEN WRITTEN WITH LOVE, THE SAME LOVE THAT UPLIFTS OUR SOULS AND MAKES THE WORLD A BETTER HOME TO LIVE IN.

I AM María Ortíz, AND I Love You...

Hello, my name is María.

I thank you in advance for taking the time to read this work.

We will focus on the positive aspects of these marvelous beings, Called Men.

Giving thanks to God for them… so, let's begin:

We will talk about these seven points:

1. From babies to elders.
2. Family role.
3. The Professional Man.
4. With adjectives.
5. The Artists.
6. The funny thing.
7. The unforgettable.

"A MAN IS A COMPLETE BEING, A WONDERFUL CREATION. HE HAS WITHIN HIMSELF EVERYTHING TO GUIDE US, SUPPORT US, HELP US WITH HIS EXAMPLE, HIS COMPASSION, HIS DELIVERY, HIS WORK AND HIS STRENGTH. THEY ARE MADE OF A RESISTANT MATERIAL, THAT ENDURES EVERYTHING, AND A SPIRIT THAT DOESN'T GIVE UP, UNTIL TO THE LAST DAY OF HIS LIFE."

FROM BABIES TO ELDERS

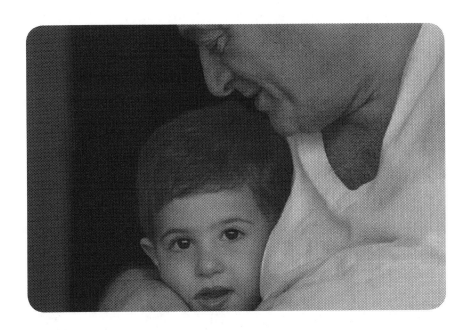

The Male Baby

There is a difference in receiving a life as male or female. Both are blessings, and you are grateful that they are healthy, as it happens in the majority of cases. But is a great happiness when your desire has been fulfilled, and yes! It's a Little Boy!

From the male baby are expected great things:

It inherits the surname, the hopes of the family to continue shining, through him. Strength is infused, because of curse, it's a Little man and they are strong. Their anatomy and physical composition develops stronger by nature. And in this difference of having a penis or vagina there is a hole variety of behavior. When they are little there is no big difference in how they behave, both sexes are lovely.

Since their first giggles, the way they sleep, the sounds that they do, the way they react to baths or showers, however you call it, it's a privilege to enjoy this new lives, no matter if you are a family member or not.

How many times we see babies in every place that they simply make us smile and surprise us with everything that they do at an early age. And you think for yourself: "I also was a baby"

Already walking

How wonderful, he started to do his first steps, he is now in the following phase, now be careful because he will do his special Little sound to call you whenever he doesn't have anything to grab from to stay still, being able to stand up or has fallen for going in such of rash, just as it keeps happening to us in the adult age. Oh God, how beautiful is the human being.

Already runs and plays

Here is where changes in the personality are noticed for male and female, the male perhaps will play with trucks and the female will cuddle her dolls, at the time of the fights, maybe she cries more because we tell him that he is a man and should not cry so much. And then we complain because they are not expressive and appear to be hard in situations of pain, if they bring it from parenting. That is how we taught them to be.

Even the mothers that can complain of Dad, brothers, the couple or men in general.

When we have a male baby and we hear him cry we tell him that he is strong, he is a man and that it has already happened, and we do what we can to bring back his smile, from there beautiful women comes the ability of men to overcome situations more easily, while we keep crying until we understand that we must move forward.

Already goes to School

Who remembers the first day of school? Some of little ones were happy for being their first day, but others did not want to stay at school, they almost had to be dragged screaming nooo or calling Mama, Papa, Nanny or the person that dropped them off that day, but they came out with a happier face and if they did well they even got a star on the forehead.

So runs his childhood, suddenly around eight or ten years old he says to you: I do not want to go to school, please, could I not go today?

And you say: Do you feel sick?

He says that he is just tired and today he only wants to sit at home, so you realize that your child is growing, he knows how to make decisions, you explain to him that he has a responsibility to fulfill, it's only hard until you shower and you will feel fine… and he says: please, I don't want to go today.

You let him rest and everything stays more or less as you expect it, but, arrives the teen age. Here is a real challenge, because he now behaves aggressive, asks you the how and the why of everything, want to do his will at the expense of everything, not really caring for anyone else, besides himself, and you say: Where did my little boy go? That one that was sweet, smiling, fun, charming and the one that was not worried about his physical appearance.

He left behind the Girls

Now he spends hours in front of the mirror, on the computer or cellphone, checking what it is fashionable, wants to drive a car to be able to invite them to go out. You are worried about he might feel ready to have sex, even though you already talked to him about the topic, but, would you be taken seriously? And what if he brings a new baby home, if this young man does not give you the feeling of being ready to be a Dad?

And what about drugs? The influences of friendships, the social pressure of this time and you became a detective using all your creativity to protect and take care of him and conserve him alive.

With God's favor you may save him and be able to help him become the responsible man who is so appreciated by everyone.

He is going to be a Dad

What? What happened? He took several sexuality classes at school, you signed all agreements for those making sure he knew more than less to be informed and be sexually careful, you made sure to answer all of his questions, you were asking quite of often if he had any questions, he kept saying no., he said once: "I think I know more than you do now". Your face of surprise was priceless...he probably looked into the media, for sure that he spent hours talking about the subject with his friends. All kinds of questions came to your mine since if he was drunk, to if he is ready for responsible parenting.

There will be some that Yes, you will be surprised that a young age they are happy and accept to work and make the necessary changes to take care of their new family, perhaps even moving to another city or country... maybe they will not return to see you soon or you will hear from them only if they need help or the relationship becomes difficult to cope with.

This separation will break your heart with a huge pain, because he is your son. But as time passes you will understand that he has to live his own life, as some time ago and perhaps even younger than him, you decided to make yours and that you felt capable of doing so. Even with all the difficulties that are not expected, it will be times in which, just like you, he will feel happy and wouldn't change himself by anyone.

And there will also be those parents who will run faster than athletes, upon hearing the news, they will also need our comprehension and not to mention the future mom and her family. We will have the choice of support and understanding in their situation, making them understand that there is a reason for everything that happens to us, and sometimes learning involves accepting the generous help of all those beautiful beings who enjoy helping others with money, friendship, support and opportunities. We all know people like that and they are famous, in addition.

At this stage we will all grow, we will have to focus, on us, and now what do I do, which is the best thing I can do at the moment, you will always see a little ray of light show up, will be your understanding that will tell you: Accept the change and continue, you can bless the good content in that situation, you can say: "It's for good, I bless the good that it contains" and you will see the good appear. (Like Conny Mendez said).

Even something as difficult as the death of a loved one. You had not wanted that they lived in pain, your love and compassion would have left them to rest, because our nature is love.

He became a Responsible Man

He already has a good job, is doing well, is moving ahead with his family and now calls you happy and grateful for all your teachings, even helps you economically, now you know that has been worth all your effort, maybe you don't need his money, but knowing that he is generous, makes you feel pride and satisfaction. Moreover, he may also help others, he developed his talents and you begin to see and hear him strong and capable, **he is around his thirties** and feels self-secure, strong, he is so charming that women fall in love with him and then he doesn't know what to do. It would be so easy to try them all and then, what could he lose? Would family be valuable, the respect of others, the professional achievements, will it affect any area or perhaps he will be forgiven?

For sure that it is not easy to be a man, above all understanding that there are many beautiful women and lovely in every way, smart, self-secure, talented and sexy if they are determined to be. The man is influenced by all of this, and Yes, sometimes fails, most couple separations and divorces happen around this age, because both men and women feel self-secure, know what they want and need, know how to get it and that causes conflicts in couples.

Everyone at some point in our lives have been attracted to someone that it is not our couple and there in that variety of circumstances is when we have to decide and learn from our circumstances, sometimes we cannot decide and someone else decides for us. Here come life changes and we have to do the best we can, according to our strength of will and the help that we allow ourselves to receive.

Perhaps we will be raising children as single parents, or simply be isolated or alone for a period of time, or return to live with the family, as in many cases. But at some time passes each one takes the reins of their life and moves forward. The men usually return to intercourse in a short time, it costs more to women, for obvious reasons, women can have more children, more responsibilities and there is fear about if it will work this time. Men on the other hand are those who propose and feel more secure and it is well known that they make decisions faster than women.

Around the Forties

At this stage grey hairs begin to appear, wrinkles are more noticeable, there are changes in the skin and the body that affect the self-esteem of men, hair loss, the speed with which they gain weight, the disadvantage that feels of being less attractive compared with the younger, the differences in sexual activity make them enter in a desperate fight with themselves. Many seek couples around twenty years old to feel that they are still attractive, presume them as if they were a trophy, change their way of dressing, many at this age seek exercise, maintain a healthy life and perhaps will be looking better than ever, if they are persistent.

Their physical appearance will help them cope with the depression that causes unfavorable changes. At this age I recommend that if one of them asks you for help, help him to accept and love himself it as he is, is very common to look like our parents or an older member of the family, this is completely normal. All somehow expect that we will, it is just that we do not know how much and how soon that may happen... I think it is a kind of nervous shock when you realize, you say to yourself; "I'm getting old."

There will be men who are contented with their looks and accept themselves as they are, even more it will not affect them as much especially if they are raising teenage kids, being a challenge for them and the rest of the family, at this age also men will have a better concept about women for the fact of seeing the situations women go through, not to mention the pain of giving birth to a son, he will see them fight and develop in all areas, even in the labor that long time ago were more for men, like construction workers.

This understanding and respect for them will be helpful in placing man in their place and be the protector that he was taught to be, their desire to protect and take care of his family and interests will make him be less focus on him and more on his priorities, perhaps he may be looking to study something new, a language, learning to play an instrument, trying to win a promotion in his work area, be more spiritual or go on a vacation, enjoy life a little more, because as he have seen, advances very quickly.

It is very likely that he is trying to rebuild his life, if so; there are many possibilities to accomplish the purposes due to the acquired maturity and committed mistakes, if this is your case, blessings.

We all have something that we always wanted to be or do and for one reason or another it was forgotten or was being postponed, for various reasons, around forty many people have a good income and can enjoy the opportunities and if they are intelligent, perhaps they don't even require much effort or money to achieve a dream. Everything is in as the song of Diego Torres says:

♪Know that it can be, believe that it will, take out our fears, pull them out. Painting the face color of hope, tempt the future with the heart... ♫

Around the Fifties

At this age may be less or more responsibilities in their lives, according to their decisions, there is less need of being physically attractive, many men just want to enjoy their life because they realize their peers with different misery and diseases, if they are aware they may want to avoid all that and if not they will already be dealing with prostate checks, high cholesterol, kidney, liver, heart attack problems.

This is the age of grandparents, also and at the same time many say goodbye to their parents, they are between welcomes and farewells, which makes them beautiful inside, they become more compassionate and loving, take life more calmly, but with the great desire that their experience helps others, enjoy giving advice and do it although not being asked to do so, their wisdom makes them nice and intuitive.

Now is not the same to get a job, since many have their own business or occupation which allows them to survive or live very well according to their talents and what they like to do. We are all good for something and that something at some point may not result in material compensation, it may still help us in some way, there are people who are happy making others happy and that is highly admirable.

I saw a quote recently by Mario Moreno (Cantinflas) saying:

"The first duty of man is to be happy,
the second is to make others happy."

Around Sixties

The desire for rest and physical and emotional wear and tear have many want to withdraw, live out of their pension and the help of the family, if possible. There are many considered children helping their parents not only with money, but doing something for them, like washing their clothes, take them to walk, to a doctor's visit and anything that is needed, you don't have to be family member to help the people of the third age. There are opportunities here for everyone to help, even being patient if they already don't listen well.

There are men who surprise us with their flat abdomen, with their wives with body of temptation, with all their money, the trucks they drive and the lifestyle they lead. No doubt they draw attention. But there is also the simple man who is content with little and has a face of satisfaction and that contagious laughter that makes us enjoy sharing with them.

They are in turn wiser and many with their mental faculties working great, will have many stories to tell and you will notice their joy when they know that they got your attention. These grandparents may still be protective and represent respect for the family, meaning that they are leaving their legacy through the younger. We began to lose more of them for so many reasons, they make us cry with their goodbye, because many times we weren't ready, they were healthy and the unexpected happened.

Around Seventies

They will tell you their favorite stories over and over again and even if your mind says: He already told me that one, your heart will say:

"Let him laugh, he doesn't even have teeth anymore."

Oh blessed grandparents, because they do not feel much-needed for bathing or combing, moreover because there won't be much to styling, you will see them using wigs, funny hats, berets of all types, lotions with scented wood, antique jewelry and if you ask them about them they will give you interesting stories, perhaps they may come from parents or grandparents. There are those who survive to older age and still teach us with their example. We all know someone.

Thanks to my Son Natanael

For teaching me what is a baby male, for all the moments I enjoyed when he was a kid, teaching him whatever came to my mind, playing with him and the happiness of enjoying his love. For having had to grow fast at seven years of age trying to understand why his parents separated. He let me see all the pain that he felt. He looked at me with such compassion that I could not do more than cry and hug him.

He grew to his thirteen between two homes, with a shared custody, then by decision of his father to go to another country, he stayed with me. Only to come to teach me what a loving being, intelligent, compassionate he is, he knows what he wants and does not change it for more, nor less. Until he gets it. He knows to endure the difficulties and is completely grateful when he gets help or is surprised with something that he has been wanting to buy. He still hugs the same way as a child and still cries of emotion of being so beloved.

He was such a big help when my son Alex was born. Due to Alex's Dad absence, he took care of Alex as if it was his own child.

He told baby Alex once: Don't worry, am going to be here for you, am going to be your Dad.

I said: It's okay Son, you don't have to be a Dad for him, don't take responsibilities that are not yours, being a Big Brother is good enough.

I've been very picky with him and we have had conflicts many times. I hope very much and the best. And when he feels pressed he fights me and makes me examples of other young people. And I say: "He is not my Son". I know what you are made of, you have been made and raised with lots of love, and I expect lots of good from you. He just smiles and hugs me again. I love him.

FAMILY ROLE

The Older Son

Who has had the blessing of being the first son of any relationship knows that he is the immediate hope to keep alive the surname, be heir and administrator of the possessions, take care of women and children at cape and spade, the first-born is usually responsible because of the pressure and the need to take care of children. They tend to be very responsible parents in adulthood, they keep feeling responsible for the hole family, react annoying when a family member is hurt and want to move Heaven and Earth to help him.

If the firstborn has a strong personality he will be the family leader after or in the absence of parents, much will be expected from him and the high expectations will make him self-demanding.

He will want to plan the holidays, will have tips for the career to choose, will want to avoid headaches and setbacks that he already exceeded, but of course, no one learns the lesson at the head of others, for that he has his own. As said by my Aunt Ignacia.

The Sandwich

It is that child between the Oldest and the Little one. This will take the pressure of both and will be influenced by the two being at any time as one or the other. As bigger the number of brothers between, there will be more variety and influence in sandwich siblings. What I find beneficial, because of the proximity of learning and being a family.

Wanting to help a sandwich I would say to help him to work on his self-esteem, to let him make decisions by himself and to support him if it does not result to be beneficial. (This does not include let him take vices or anything else that could damage him, of course he will be cared for). When he gets confidence in himself he will not need to resemble anyone.

The Little One

This son is normally protected and cared for by everyone in the family. I also believe that they tend to be handsome or attractive since they are much told they are, for the reason that he is still the baby of the family and are always seen as beautiful by being the youngest.

This son as a couple tends to be playful, as if he was still a child. Does not feel the need to control and makes the relationship to be bearable. They suffer no need for love, since they had much and seek relationships where they feel protected and accepted.

Thanks to my Son Alexander

For being my youngest son at this time of life, for his constant company. Because since he was born I do not feel alone, for being my life partner at this time. For making me a better person because I know that he needs me. For all the kisses and hugs when he sees me cry, because his little character comes out and tells me that all will be well, that don't worry.

We can talk all day about how much we love each other, sometimes I ask him if he can give me a kiss and he says Yes, but he approaches his cheek so I kiss him. And when I get a no, I would tickle and hug him and tell him it's okay, that I love him and he is very handsome. He is like an Angel to me in these moments of my life.

The Uncle

They are those brothers from Mom and Dad. Even cousins of them. The uncles sometimes treat as if they were our parents and advise us with affection. They also serve as examples to follow if we like how they behave or we see a result that we want for us. They tend to be protective, especially if they are asked to care for the family on the death of the Dad.

My brother came to visit a couple of months ago and while he was at home was very loving with my son Alex. He was telling him that his haircut was nice and that he wanted his hair. A few weeks later I told Alex that Uncle Emilio was coming to our house and that we needed to go to get a haircut, he accepted with no claims. He was happy that Uncle Emilio was coming.

Other times it had been difficult to convince him to go up to the Chair, had troubles in getting him to be still and calm while the Barber worked, this time he was still. At the end of the haircut he touched his hair, smiled and thanked. He took my hand and said to me: I'm ready for Uncle Emilio.

The Cousin

It is very nice to share with the cousins, because they are seen and loved as brothers in many cases and even when there are no own brothers. Normally we trust them, unless they have failed us. It is also a competitive relationship being beneficial if you want to improve.

When Children we feel them as our best friends, there may be many fights, but when there are moments of happiness the hugs are genuine and the shouts of euphoria are authentic.

The Grandfather

He may be the favorite of the family. Thanks to his ability to give and receive love. Grandparents have a lot to teach us and see us with compassion if we make a mistake. There will be times in which they will want to help us and others that they will respect our decisions, especially if it's something in which they were not let able to choose.

Grandparents would like to have eaten more ice cream, because their teeth were damaged anyway, would not have been worried so much, if they had known that they would have a long life. They would have danced more, because just the same their knees hurt, laughed more, because equal their skin is wrinkled.

They desire they had loved more their absent loves and want to help you become a grandparent so or happier than they are.

The Uncle Grandpa

This one sees us with love, enjoys our company and compares us with his family to check if his influence is positive. And he will also observe through us the inheritance of our parents and our use of it. He will want to help us if we are important to him or at any time he may need our help.

He will feel weird if you run and embrace him with love, or look for his advice, will appear surprised. But his memory and heart will keep those moments that pass so quickly, but they are so cute.

THE PROFESSIONAL MAN

The Teacher

He is that being that has studied and has been prepared and trained himself before teaching us.

They cause admiration, especially if at any time we wanted to be one of them. You must be patient to be a teacher, since many times the students don't want to learn or are not ready to receive the teaching. He may need to teach the same lesson many times and will get frustrated to see that there are still people who are not interested in or pass an examination. It is as if his work lacks importance.

But when he sees his positive achievements he knows it has been worth it and moves on. These people do not get tired of teaching. I read recently the story of master Buddha and said that when he was about to die, he met his disciples informing them that his hour had come and that if someone had a question to do it. Everyone felt sad and nobody dared to ask, so he asked twice more, to what someone asked: Why question three times? and Buddha replied: "Because sometimes the mind does not react to the first call."

The Doctor

No matter the area of health this man has the gift of healing, the compassion to understand that many times we don't take care as we should, to understand that on many occasions we do not have the resources and that people live as they can or survive.

Almost all of us have been assisted by a doctor, even before we were born. It is a very blessed profession if you ever want to be one of them. For sure that will not fail to work, nor to have opportunities to save lives with your learning and lifestyle. And you can also inspire others to follow you.

I follow a doctor on a social network, he is also a speaker and his tips have helped me a lot. I use him as guide when I need a healthy answer to which I'm living and his advices are helpful because they focus on the general well being.

The Lawyer

This man has the intelligence to retain lots of information, since laws are always changing. From an age of student, he is subject to many tests and will have to pass them all at the end for his title, and be registered at the bar of lawyers. He has its specific branch and he must know a little of the others to advise his clients and give recommendations of colleagues.

For a lawyer to fight a case brings into play his credibility and capability of achievement. When there is a case in which there is an opponent lawyer is as if it was a boxing bout. Even the arrive on time for a meeting is important. He is a very self-demanding person, since his achievements will allow him to best income, also the recognition of his peers and the satisfaction of knowing that has done so well.

There are lawyers who are also engaged in defending human rights and take up the fight as if they actually stood up for a family member. They will get many achievements and satisfactions since their orientation is to help since the beginning. Blessings for them and thank you for their work.

The Judge

This man has the ability to decide in many different cases, taking into account all the people involved and all of the information provided. He will focus us on being to the point and want clear-cut answers, no doubt. There will be occasions in that the cases take long time to get resolved and others in which perhaps will be reopened, but he will continue to work according to his principles, his ideals and will apply his experience in each situation.

He is worthy of admiration due to his responsibility of deciding on matters of money, children, changes of residence in adults or deprive people of liberty. Can even influence in laws that are in process of approval and help to continue forward if are to benefit a large number of people.

The Police Officer

This man is a human being braver than many, risks his life many times and is exposed to difficult circumstances that sometimes he cannot get out of his mind. I work as a waitress at a breakfast restaurant and we have several police officers as customers.

A few days ago I met Mike and we talked about the issue and he told me that that night he had a fight. I asked if he felt fear and he said that two more officers were with him, at the time he did not feel fear. It was then when was out of the job and remembered the weapons and the danger in which he was. I asked if he could sleep and if they had some kind of therapy or if he relied on the family to overcome it, or preferred not to mention work to not affect them.

He told me that sometimes he couldn't sleep, had a companion of housing who was also police officer. But they were kept busy and preferred not to mention work because it eats you, according to him. He said had his Dad and that he could talk to him in any situation. And Yes, that they had therapy and can go for check up and they could relax until they were ready to return to work.

Although I know that sometimes injustices happen with the police. I'm also aware that they are necessary in many circumstances and put order in our lives and as I said at the beginning, we are focusing on the positive aspects.

The Firefighter

When we think of firefighter a young man with a good musculature and attractive comes to mind. Thanks to the calendars made by firefighters. Although in reality there are all types it is well known that they are trained to have a physical condition and save lives.

They maintain in good condition their hoses and the truck that must be ready in case of emergency. The truth is that you have to be very brave to not be afraid to fire and exit in aid of persons and animals in some cases. Not to waste time on the way to your mission and get used to the sound of the siren while in the assigned rescue. It must be nice to change traffic lights to green, although even they perhaps do this to go to their rest and meal. Anyway, his profession is required for our society.

The Entrepreneur

This man has the ability to create companies, to guide many people, has the ability to delegate responsibilities, he is a leader with vision of giving opportunity to many people, to compete with the best and not get discouraged when the project does not go as he hopes. His vision of winner makes him find solutions to all what is presented. He will also have his priorities as a family, but being the boss or the business owner will give him the reward to take the time for his needs. He will want to leave an inheritance for his loved ones and if he has to close or stop a project feels satisfied from the experience and will only do better at the beginning of his new project.

Interested in their appearance and they look after it with good clothing and whether in all what they use give you the image of power, there are simple ones also who do not want to draw attention. But I think it is intelligent not only be, but look alike who you are. Above all, if they are looking for new opportunities. And then of course, is everyone's choice.

The Administrator

To this man is given the trust of money, decisions, and people who work in the business. There are also administrators on the family. Even in couples is recommended to leave the task to those who know better how to manage money. But if the couple is a man and woman, the man will hardly accept that women do so. Especially if it is his money, the man was trained to be a leader. For that reason, women should care for their words and give him the confidence that the suggestions are for the good of the family and not her's only.

Turning to the employment area, this type of man is organized, very thinking because he has to make decisions constantly. Looks for the best way to negotiate and the right words to bring the feast in peace, as far as possible.

We all know someone like that and often cause envy by the trust that is placed in them, but well, many times they deserve it.

The Social Worker

This man knows that he should use the services available in favor of others, instructs people to learn how to apply and obtain benefits. He is in the midst of the need and the abundance what makes him a wise being and compassionate at the same time. His work is tedious because he has to receive and review many documents, dealing with many people in a single day.

If there is a busy person, they are. Carrying dates, making calls, verifying information and working with this pile of folders, that are waiting to be reviewed. The gratitude of all beneficiaries makes that at the moment this person needs something will be someone to help him.

The Chef

Many of us have had pleasant experiences with a Chef who cooked even better than our Grandma, I admire them the ability to cook so quickly, how they decorate the plates.

The male released that Yes, long ago were women in charge of the kitchen, now many men cook and are not ashamed of that. They see it as a decent job thanks to the recognition they receive, in my job you can see them and many times when a client or guest says goodbye, gives thanks to the Chef and is nice to see their smile. We all like to be recognized.

The Server and Bartender

Although it does not sound to profession, more to an occupation, in tourist cities like Las Vegas, people prepares and takes classes to serve alcohol, and gets trained to give the best possible service. Preparation and patience is required to deal with tourists and locals too, of course. People are accustomed to the special treatment since most have family or friends who are dedicated to the service.

Serve is an exhausting experience as it muddles through the energy and emotions of many people at the same time. There is too much pressure, many times people are demanding and not considered, although they see a very busy place. Sometimes they arrived in quantity at the same time and people serving only makes the possible for not neglecting anyone. There is nothing personal against anybody, nor preference. Only people with very large ego who think that they should be dealt with before the others.

Often they are seen as money-hungry, since they receive tips. But in fact in many cases their salary is the minimum and not all people give tips. But they know that will compensate ones with others. There is generous people who will make any of this people's day.

They deal with people from all social levels and although sometimes are treated as servants, they must be respectful, control their emotions, even smile and thank at the end. They thank you if you pay the Bill, although not to leave a tip. There are people who leave without paying and others that do not cover the account completely and this is only a headache more in the day. As the returns of a food up to three times because the guest did not like it, sounds as if is not a great thing. But the food is given away in many of the complaints, when it is busy it makes to hold longer the following orders.

Serving as well is a privileged position. You have many opportunities to fulfill the spiritual question: "How may I serve"?

The Architect

This man has the ability to realize dreams, makes the drawing with the exact measurements and convert this little work to as large as required. He has a clear vision of creator that increases with his opportunity to work, learns and practices with each of them. He gets excited when he passes through a place and sees an already completed creation which knows that he did and feels satisfaction for the time spent and everything what had to be done to achieve what now can be seen in physical.

This people are self-secure thanks to their job is well paid. But they can also be generous and give a drawing as a wedding gift, I happened to see it up close. It was certainly nice and appreciated, not only in the moment. Is still recalled thanks to the service that has given through the years. Because the project was built gradually.

The Gardener

I see them very often here working on the property where I live, many of them are Mexicans or Hispanics. It's a humble job. But, there are people with the ability to be simple. These men can revive and change color to virtually everything they touch.

They have the patience to wait for the flowers, collect leaves and deal with the winter, where his work is not very necessary. They are kept busy meanwhile doing what they like, as play soccer, dance, enjoy their days off and if they have money saved they can pay their expenses with the little work that comes up, they are also open to do other related work as concrete, cleaning pools, help you move and whether all that see opportunity to work.

Thanks to their humble condition none type of work embarrasses them. They get ashamed of not having enough money even to invite you to eat. They are simple men, but they surprise you when they dress up. They can look very well.

WITH ADJECTIVES

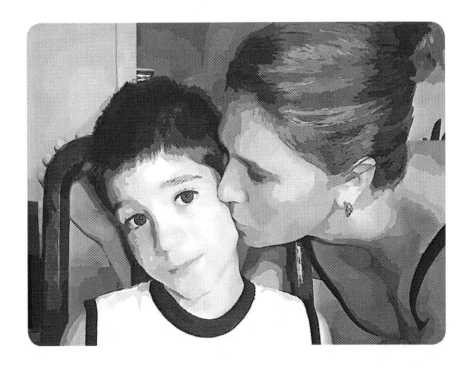

Probably my favorite writing section. While I write in my kitchen table, my youngest son is beside me watching a film of spider man on his Tablet and feeding me with his spoon. Far from distracting me causes me happiness. It's nice to be in the company.

The Funny Guy

This man finds the way to have fun wherever he is. An ex-coworker told me that her oldest son was difficult to discipline, since he didn't care if he was punished or took away something that he liked, as a toy, video game, television or anything else in which he showed being happy. He always found the way to have fun even there in his corner.

"It was difficult to steal his happiness," she said. What made smile the two of us. I admire people who have the ability to have fun in boring places, at work and in the situations of life where many times we get frustrated, as in relationships.

This funny man puts humor and good face to what he lives and that makes him someone very pleasant when looking for company or friendship.

Even they are examples to follow in diseases. They have the ability to tell jokes and laugh with them, even more they laugh at themselves.

The Positive

This man is smiley, kind, compassionate. It gives encouragement to those who need it, he tries to get you out of sad feeling by telling you other stories more difficult than yours. Even his own experiences. He gives you one and a thousand solutions to having a positive attitude. He helps you to not take things so to heart.

One of his phrases will be that "the best is yet to come" and you say well hopefully, God wants, and he says: cheer up man, everything passes. Then you're going to laugh at this. For a good reason things are or are not happening. Teaches you to ask and be open to receive what you asked or something better. And convince you that you're worthy of it. And if you're hard head he finds the way to make you smile.

The Handsome

This man is responsible for many sighs during his lifetime. His physical appearance, its form of grooming, personal hygiene, the flirtatious smile and that pleasant smell make him look as handsome. There are men who are not so handsome physically, but their behavior makes them very pleasant or they are so neat and smell so delicious that somehow they are perceived as handsome.

This man causes a stir wherever he goes, is usually someone confident, though realistically there are many good-looking. Each one has its possibilities of advancement and usually knows where can achieve something. Although there are some arrogant that to hear that they are handsome from someone they not care for, behave unattainable.

I don't think a nice comment from someone will go further than personal taste or maybe that day the whole person looked good, probably reminds you of someone you know. So handsome, please, be careful with your reactions, you might miss the opportunity to meet nice people in any way.

The Don Juan

This man has a surprising ability to conquer women. His adventurous spirit makes him get bored easily of the accomplished conquest and sees a challenge to meet in a new relationship. This man is not intimidated for being short, dark skin, quietly, can be potbelly, alcoholic, not well educated but he is confident in himself and in his ability of conquest that is even inspiring others, as the timid, that if at some point are interested in someone will take the advice of Don Juan.

This man hardy falls in love, as is constantly distracted by what there is on the menu, that he doesn't focus or connects completely sentimentally to the couple of the moment. Likes to have sex, and the only way that you will be a little more important for him is if you have his son. He will remember you, but it will be more by the sexual relationship that made that child being formed. This man enjoys company while he has it, because life which is also wise teaches him that there are more available men and sometimes loses his best person for Security surplus.

While this seems to be something negative it is not. Many times we spent pleasant moments and they do not last for a long time. And it is in that variety of experiences that we take the most suitable with ourselves or our interests. And if you've fallen in love with a Don Juan, give thanks to God that is love.

The Sexual Machine

This man enjoys sexual intercourse a lot, due to his ability to perform it. Knows exactly where to touch, is very active and can last for hours having sexual intercourse without getting tired, he even smiles so much that is noticeable that he enjoys it. This type of man is usually also very fertile, very easy and quick can get a woman pregnant. So you will have to take care of yourself if it is not your desire or is in your future plans to create a new life.

This type of man will revolutionize the idea you had in your mind about sex, will make you analyze your past relationships and inevitably will compare your old loves with him. Your preference will place you where you want to be. But in the place that is if you see it positive you will appreciate the experience and now won't be impressed easily by other partners, more if they don't have good performance in bed and this quality is important, you will tend to find someone more suitable to you. We all come to the world with different talents and the sexual man machine has been who has caused unforgettable experiences and new lives, in many cases.

The Understanding

This type of man has the ability to get in the shoes of the other person, they are very good advisors. Personally I think we all know who to go in every situation when we need help. And I have received many of the top tips of my male friends. Many times they tell you what you don't want to hear, but it will make you see the situation in a different way and sometimes it will simply help you to listen to them.

My father died when I was two years old, that's why I had no experiences of his education or example that I can remember, only anecdotes from my mother saying that he was a good man and the food he liked. So I appreciate the understanding and care giving of sympathetic men. They are loving people who find pleasure in helping who requested their help, but smart to not get involved if they may be affected. Because they are sympathetic with them, but they know that they must take care of one's own or if not also will be looking for help to recover what is important to them.

Thanks to everyone understanding, that sometimes when they've been told, or know of any situation, their gestures or laughter expresses so much that they do not even need to speak to express and let you know that they understand you and you will have to go ahead, it will be worth it.

The Innocent

If you've had the experience of meeting an innocent man, you're going to remember him here. There is a blessing in innocence, it is that beautiful thing that we have when we are children. There are men who have been able to keep it at an adult age, aged between thirty and forty, and even at an older age.

The innocent man believes many times things that are not true, his mind does not think that something is being told with bad intentions or desire to harm him or fool him. Reacts many times as a child to life situations that he could even cause you desperation.

But wait, don't run in such of hurry... innocence often saves us from evil, because the purpose which was intended to make often fails. It could even up to perhaps benefit rather than harm him.

When he talks to someone dear and explains any living situation, might be the dear one convinces him that there were bad intentions and he realizes that it is true, due to the consequences. He'll want to then put distance, and learn from what happened.

For example, if he is convinced of stealing, it does and it were jailed, beaten or damaged in any way, would be someone who will save him or will benefit in some way. Because he did it in innocence, not in malice.

We should think twice about wanting to harm anyone innocent. They are valuable human beings and we do not want to pay the consequences of stealing, mistreat him, mock him or fail to understand him. Sometimes we need to see our fellow men with eyes of love and the innocent will make you exercise this virtue.

The Generous Men

This type of man donates his talents and money for the benefit of others. My oldest son recently met a man who works in real estate. The man said he liked his personality and that saw him future at that branch. My son is young and hesitated to trust him. The man suggested that if he could be hired by his boss, he would train him for six months and will teach him all that he has learned. He said be a millionaire at the age of 30. It may be that this is someone generous.

One of my teachers that I follow made a recent video (Dr. Wayne Dyer) where he talks of the soul callings to help others. He admitted that there is a teller at the Bank he assists which helps with two hundred dollars whenever he goes. Because he knows that her husband is ill and she has to sustain him and their kids. He also goes to a laundromat where he takes cash to a woman with overweight and her husband is unemployed. He feels that these two families now depend of him somewhat. He also said that when his children come to visit they like cash, so he goes to the Bank and withdraws cash for them.

He called burning desires to the need to help others. The sense of responsibility and the joy that feels to relieve the needs of others. Without a doubt an example to follow.

Thanks to Mr. Manny

For having changed my life to have been chosen as a wife. For Let me live with his family and get to know other lifestyle, different from my family, more economically disadvantaged, but with more household. Because the wanting to help them made me try a thousand solutions. Because I could be a good influence in their lives. That made me grow as a person and I realize that my talents were appreciated and grateful.

For bringing me from Mexico to Las Vegas. I love this city... for the change of life and consciousness that brought to my life. Here was born my son Nate, we changed his life also. I had to learn English, deal with many different jobs, learn from many different cultures and the message was the same: do not give up and move forward.

He supported and helped me to learn, he suffered when he saw me getting pretty to go to work and have to see me messy at home. He used to hug me for long time when I got home, and listened to my talk of how my day went, with patience, although he was very tired.

He treated me in such of nice way that is hard to match on people I have meet the last years. I know that there is many beautiful souls. I can tell that he is one of them. I was able to see that purity of heart and so much love on his eyes, even though I can also see in those eyes that he has been suffer so much in his life. Thank you for being there for me and for being someone I have to love without conditions, for letting me see how difficult life was at times. But God always helped us and sent Angels as people, to help us solve it all. As of miracle.

THE ARTISTS

The Sculptor

This man mold with his hands everything he touches. Whether by personal taste or project in which he is working, he dedicates his work the necessary time. No matter how many times he has to repair it, to improve parts and make all the necessary changes until the new creation is finished.

His example teaches us to treat different materials, forms, and to use the creator inventive in many different creations that someone will do theirs. That no matter how long they last complete. But that they had been created to be admired, beloved. Each with its purpose to accomplish, no matter how long they last. As human beings, we are created the same way. Thanks to the Creator.

The Writer

This man has had the blessing to be able to teach forgotten data, new teachings, stories of all kinds: educational, recreational, humorous, informative, social, critical. To mention a few. We captivate with their poems and much more with their songs. They entertain us and are even able to heal broken hearts, make us laugh, cry, and move us with what they write. Technology now makes audiobooks, books that can be purchased and stored in computers and all these smart devices that every day surprise us more and more and which are becoming necessary and accessible to the community.

Social networks promote all types of materials and we have scope to much information that prepares us more for future experiences, I admire the love with which many men write. The generosity to share their writings free of charge. The desire to help a lot of people wining only the satisfaction of serve.

Also written plays, comedies, series, movies, documentaries and many more creations that help us to cope with the stress of everyday life, concerns and they also can make people forget their diseases, even if it's only for few moments.

The Musician

It is very nice to enjoy the music. There are so many men throughout history that have dedicated themselves to be musicians. It is even their way of providing well being. Many times they don't sleep at night due to the events that are more commonly at night and those who come to have success travel more. Sometimes they feel sadness for feeling that they abandon those that they love, but all that sadness is expressed in love when playing that or those instruments which make them vibrate. They Enjoy it so much that in reality time moves so fast that sometimes do not realizes until it has to finish, even if the listener asks to hear more.

The adrenaline is huge. More even if it is a large public. And even with a small one, a person, or for himself finds satisfaction in what he makes and continues learning as he practices more and more of the already learned. The talent is appreciated and rewarded very generously on many occasions due to the well being that causes. In this way this man also helps to provide a better experience of life to the people that he has contact with.

The opportunity of playing comes with entertaining and many times comes accompanied with alcohol, drugs or sex. There is a tremendous difficulty in maintaining values, the family united and to the integrity of the man himself, especially if it has a tendency to enjoy these practices. You have to be living in love, albeit self-respect to resist the excesses and maintain a healthy life.

The Singer

Everyone at some point in our lives have been identified with the music. The form of expression of the singer makes us vibrate, laugh, dance, sing and there are songs that stay with us as special experiences. As memories that are not forgotten. Sometimes remind us of someone beloved with whom we enjoyed a certain piece. Or they describe the personality of someone important for us.

The singers have that interior strength and creativity that attracts thousands of people to any place they go. They are the busiest events often, without removing credit to sports, of course. Is as if they had magic to enchant us. Many of us have favorite singers that each new material attracts us because we simply like the singer. Resonates with our personality doesn't matter even if he changes music genre. I admire the singers that can put us the hen skin with their interpretations.

There are also those using social topics to compose songs and own experiences, what makes many people identified with them and seek more of their creations. I recently met a rap singer who is working on his second cd. The first one is played on the radio in his country, but the material didn't sell, has been given. He now works on the second cd and uses the technology to send free songs to people so they can listen to them. Perhaps at some point he may charge for his work, now he does it just for the pleasure of expressing what he lives. You start somewhere, don't you think?

There are many singers who are still successful despite their advanced age, do not cease to work. They have the ability to take care of their health and their voice and are capable of staying reliable for us. They say that they will die singing. That's when one realizes that they love to be artists.

The Painter

This man has learned to use color, imagination and skills to add color and detail to a blank sheet, to a blanket, a commercial business, a shop, a bathroom, a house, a mansion. There are so and so many development opportunities that these people have that they become passionate and are excited as they learn a new technique. There are painters who also have the ability to be cartoonists.

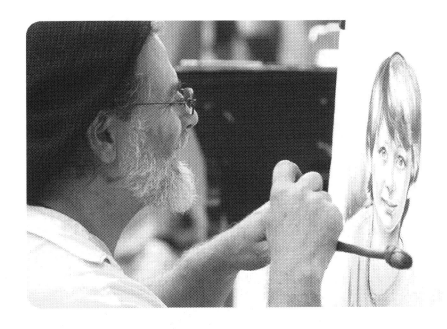

There are many famous people who have created wonderful creations and very expensive. Ancient paintings that are exhibited in museums and art galleries where there are buyers willing to purchase them regardless of the price. Picasso, Da Vinci, Monet, Van Gogh are famous examples.

Even the simple painters who paint to live, enjoy wearing their clothing usually white painted many other colors. That is what distinguish them as painters. Someone in my family was such a painter, but his clothes had no colors, was so clean to work that when he arrived at the House that he was going to paint they were surprised and asked him if he was the painter, who even looked very young.

When he finished the job received gratuities and often people called him to make more jobs for friends and family, he learned to do artwork on walls like waterfalls, rocks, a solar system, the illusion that a butterfly comes out of a broken wall and many more. His works were sold through photos organized in a folder that he will carry every time he did a new job. He got to paint at home and really he was very clean.

Covering all areas very carefully to ensure that spots were nowhere else that wasn't the work area, covering the entire floor and used shoe protectors to ensure not to step on a drop of paint and stained another floor. Also was very fast to work and his works were of good quality and clean, that was appreciated.

The Dancer

This man has the capability of expressing his feelings dancing. He may not even need music to move, has a creative mind that works even asleep. The ideas don't stop coming and he becomes better each day. Either that his dance is accompanied in couple, group, crowd or alone.

Although it has its specialty, or preference for dance, identifies other types of dance and is ethical of any dancer to know the basic steps of other rhythms, even if he doesn't use them very often. There is always someone willing to learn with them, thanks to all the benefits of dance: is a good exercise for the sensuality, health, to conquer, fall in, makes the music or the singer or the piece look better, with more meaning. It is a good addition to the personality of the man and has many advantages the ability to move with grace.

I highly recommend to men to learn to dance. Is something that we as women appreciate much. We like to let ourselves go with them and follow their steps, we enjoy the surprises to move us, sustain us, and give us the security to not let us fall. I Honestly feel that it is an advantage to know how to dance and that those men that make it with grace have more opportunities of conquest that those whom are not interested. Even it has said that improves sexual performance. A good reason to consider if you like to improve on moving better at the time of the action. Is very appreciated in dancers that take care of their body and the practice of the dance improves health and physical appearance.

The Magician

Although is not very common any more to see presentations of wizards, the magic is still being very appreciated. Disney creations, for example, from their theme parks to each creation that has been made to be seen on screen are still being watch for generations, magic captivates us and attracts many times trying to find the trick and other times we just enjoy what we see.

Technology doesn't stop surprising us, now there are screens very small and with lots of quality, similar to the magic that keeps us entertaining and admiring. The skill with which the shows are carried out makes us feel like children again, it makes us see images of dreams and no doubt smile on many occasions.

Thanks to all modern magicians who do not cease to work. By teaching us that the magic is within us, that we can use the imagination to create what we wish to see realized in our experience and move into the space that is beneficial to us, to save and be saved.

And being romantic would say that: "Love is the magic that heals all diseases".

The Model

Men have opened opportunities in all areas, it is not surprising that there are men who are interested in being models.

They have a very high self-esteem and they like the art and all that is beautiful, they like to appreciate landscapes and life in color. They enjoy being alone and in silence with them. In the stillness of spirit creativity appears and gives shape to interesting projects and magical experiences, what passionates models.

The magic of the technology makes that the creations take life. Photos and expressions of them are simply beautiful. Their bodies cause admiration and respect.

THE FUNNY THING

In this section I will narrate weird things that have happened to me with these beautiful men.

The Sexier

The sexier a man has made to me... It was a rainy night; my boyfriend had come to pick me up from work. He drove home, it was very cold and to complete the night the rain was pouring heavy, the music was nice, his voice too, it had that masculine and sensual touch that they use at the stage of conquest.

He parked the car and we stayed there speaking, the caresses in the face began, the hugs. Not to draw the attention of the neighbors we decided to go to the back seat. The temperature began to rise despite the cold, he already wanted to be intimate with me. I thought that it was not time yet.

He would provoke me wanting to hurry me and I spent tremendous work at continue to resist, this time was no exception. I was curious to see his naked body since he was very well dressed. So I asked: "can you remove the shirt"? I was not even finished asking when he pull it out immediately leaving to see a body of magazine, very well formed and with that brown skin that I like so much. His head was shaved, no doubt he didn't had a silly hair. I was surprised by the speed and security that he made it, most men need insistence to do so. And the smile that he had to do so is an expression that I don't forget.

We went to the next step, time later. Without doubt this experience encouraged me to accept.

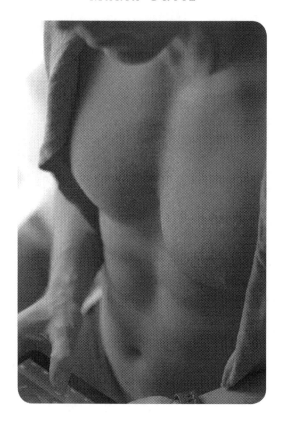

The Joke Teller

This man loved to tell jokes, had an addiction to his cell phone, a gym body and an addiction for women. He liked to carry good stereos and quality sound in his car and although on two occasions they were stolen he would go to rebuy them to look good and show that he earned good money. He liked soccer and the regional Mexican music, he used the shirts adjusted to his body that left to see a chest very well formed, his pants were also adjusted and said that women loved to touch his butt. I think that was improving his self-esteem.

There were times that he called me by phone and I didn't answer and he will not be conformed, he will dial private, will fake another voice asking for me.

He said: Don't you remember me? We met last night...

I said: Really? I didn't go out last night. Okay Carlos what do you need?...

C: Just talk to you, but you don't answer. And how do you know it's me if I speak different?

M: Because no one else thinks of faking the voice, only you...

People in a good mood is certainly nice and creative.

On one occasion he told me that he had a co-worker who had a sexual problem and was afraid that his wife will leave him. He asked this guy for advice. And my friend told him to tell her jokes, that he would make her happy that way.

C: What do you think?

M: I think that it is good idea to tell her jokes without a doubt he will make her laugh, but I don't think it will work for a long time. Sexual dissatisfaction is not a joke and your friend should be treated and save his marriage.

The Guy with Long Legs

The physical attractiveness and the personal preferences of each person to choose couple are fully understood and respected. Normally we tend to choose people that complement us or are similar to us in any way. In other cases, is just the opposite, the difference in the color of skin that I see very often in my culture, where the woman has lighter skin, short height, she can be friendly and other times very strong of character what makes forget her physical smallness. Also when it comes to making decisions and life changes.

This was the case on one of my relationships. This gentleman had long legs, passed troubles and inconveniences since bedtime, where his feet will come out the bed, and there was a need to keep an eye on him to shelter them because he experienced tremendous cold, especially in the winter season.

There were places where we lived where the intermediate walls or doors of the House were not sufficiently high and had to bend over. He spent tremendous work settling into the car at the time of going out, he had to move the chair and bend one by one his legs to be able to fit in the space, what I founded adorable when I remembered about him with sympathy. Seeing him struggle made me appreciate my difference of not having to deal with anything like that and on the other hand I saw him as a giant which protected me and would fight for me, if necessary. He had an imposing personality, a hard character with others, but gentle with me. He could not resist my caresses. Although he was upset.

It was true love for some years, I compared it as that Hulk's movie where the character was so angry that will turn green of rage, grew and became so strong that it destroyed his clothes, could fight and remove of his way everything that crossed him or tried to hurt him… and she will appear in the place of battle… Was a small female and even thin. He turned to see her and immediately began to deflate and become human again. She will come to him and they kiss. She had the gift of calm him down.

The one which melts

This man has ice cream syndrome, it melts... have you known someone who melts to your charms, which cannot resist your presence, that one that even when he is angry you have the power to steal him a smile?

This man is a charm, there is a special chemistry between you two that has the power to alter his moods, his decisions, his perception in view of the circumstances and has that weakness, that skinny side towards you or someone very dear, may be a daughter, a son, his parents. Indeed, such is its weakness when he decides something and knows that his decision can be influenced by anyone, avoids to see the person or talk or demonstrate what he plans to do, because he knows that if it does not perhaps will not achieve do his task.

It may even be that he is preparing a surprise for you, but if you realize how much money and effort represents perhaps you would say that it is not necessary and there are generous souls who know that you deserve it.

THE UNFORGETTABLE

The first kiss

The first kiss is important for many women. It is said that it's not forgotten, for men I think is most the first sexual experience. Returning to the kiss it's an experience a little strange, first because you have the fear of not knowing how to kiss and not sure what to do with the tongue when another mouth sticks to yours. There are since the nice kisses up to the disgusting ones. And we will focus on the pleasant, only to make it positive.

There is a tremendous shame especially if you have a small age, the other is the adrenaline to be seen, found and punished by the elders, making it an adventure. If you are lucky to not be interrupted gets to have meaning. It is the beginning of the union as a couple, the feeling is like entering another universe and energy other than yours. It is as if two circles merge and the merger raises energy, the famous butterflies in the stomach and the accelerated heartbeat make you want to stay there and try again.

And the first kiss is also not only the first person who kiss you but that important relationship, that important person in your life, that night of dancing and passion where the temperature went up and had to finish with a parting kiss, despite of just knowing each other that night, the night that makes intimate every moment and that is so conducive to make love.

The Brave One

There are men destined to heroic missions, they are capable of jumping in parachute, fly aircrafts, save lives. They train to serve and have the gift of being heroes. From the higher charges to beginners, many of them use uniform, others don't, they are everyday beings that help us in danger needs. As if they were angels in Earth.

It is as if they possessed a physical strength superior to that of the normal human being, and a goodness of heart that can do everything carefully and calm if required. Have the ability to control their feelings and remain focused for long time, and are even willing to give their life if necessary for the well of others. They have an unbreakable faith and an absolute goodness.

The way in which they work is worthy of being admired, their actions inspire others and they are able to steal our heart.

The Sacrificed One

There are men who came to Earth with the gift of sacrifice, often are judged as fools and yet do not let it get to them, they continue with the work of sacrifice that decided to dedicate their life. I've seen cases where the man sacrificed an unhealthy relationship with the partner, in order to not be separated from the children. I had a friend that told me his history:

My partner and I decided to divorce, but when we decided to talk to our children about the separation my children began to cry with a crying heartbreaking that split my heart. They shouted in a way that it seemed that someone had died on them.

At that moment I decided that I wasn't going to get a divorce for them. We don't even have intimacy anymore. I just do the best I can to spend time with my kids, I take them to eat at places that they enjoy. I makes me feel good to see them happy, I know that my sacrifice is worth it.

The grandparents of one of my children had a similar relationship. The husband could not live without the wife. The common thing to do for most of the men there was coming to the United States, to the North, as it is said there to work for a while and return with enough money to make life changes that benefit the family.

He had friends who invited him to go to try his luck, once his friend gave him a jacket that he brought and the gentleman was happy with it, he never had one like this, over there he wasn't earning enough that he would have extra to buy something for him, they had nine children and the responsibility was huge and due to the difference in government, salary was not enough. To worsen the poverty that they were going through, he was an alcoholic and was dissipating money in that also, money that would have improved their life.

I believe that it has to be very painful to live in poverty for many years to not dare to break away from the family, but he simply couldn't. On one occasion he took a chance and crossed the border, he struggle to find a job and had a hard time accommodating to the way of living. I know that he wanted to talk to the Lady every day, just to tell her how much he missed her. He was able to stand it only a few months and then returned.

My respect and admiration for those men that are capable of the sacrifice in any situation of life and that teach us with their example.

The Indian Blood

In my home country, Mexico. We are a mixture of Indian with Spanish, so we are called mongrels. From there come the mixtures in the looks on people of my culture. Many of us are proud of the Indian blood that we have inherited from our ancestors.

My grandparents were Indian; they were a loving couple. My grandfather had a deep respect for my grandmother, he was tall, brown skin, muscular, strongly built, he had sensual lips and compassionate eyes. My grandmother was short, light-skinned, thin lips and bright eyes, had a pretty face, I remember. Grandfather loved to kiss her, he kissed her passionately after work. She began to touch his arms and the two were happy. It was beautiful to see them together, he died before her that's why we keep the memories. She died some time ago, my mom says that she decided to stop eating, she had been in pain for a while and decided that it was time to leave. Grandma asked my mom to please watch over her little son, who was already fifty years old, and was still living with her. My mom accepted and Grandma died in peace.

I got the like of Indians from them, that brown skin, that strength, the male appeal of that man who knows how to love, to please his wife, fight for her and leave an indelible mark in the family and in society. There is a popular song that sings Banda Machos and many of us can identify with that, says:

♫ I don't live among so much poverty anymore, I live as my father dreamed. I don't ambition wealth either, the Indian blood I carry is better. ♪

Is just a way of expression of being proud and loving to whatever your family was. Anywhere you were born is a blessing that made your life show up in here. With all of us. Anywhere in the planet. We are all one.

Those Eyes

The eyes are the windows to the soul, it is said many times. It's recommended to look in the eye as a sign of care and to know if people are telling the truth. But there are times that become unforgettable.

Like those of color, who are neither brown, nor black being the most common.

When a baby is born the eyes is one of the curiosities that is more appreciated, especially if are green, blue, honey color, grey or a mix difficult to determine, seems that change of color according to the clothing that the person is wearing. It is something that does not go unnoticed.

And, how does the eyes of someone at the time of making love look like, before crying, when searched offended, when searched abused, them of goodness, of compassion, of support, of fellowship, the eyes of scoundrels, them of complicity, them of the flirtation and when you had to close them to someone that died, what did you felt, to who you remember?

No doubt that eyes are a trait imposing in the personality and there are men that we don't forget by those eyes they had. By the way that they looked at us could guess what they wanted, just that sometimes made them battle it out so they insisted to make it happen.

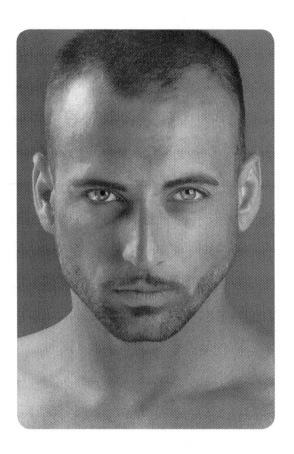

Thanks to my boyfriend Tony

For having the patience of dealing with me, my family, my feelings, for being a hero many times when I most needed a hand… whether was money, help on fixing something at home, changing the tires on my car, advise about any situation that was hard to deal with and sometimes just listening to me crying on the phone not having any other way to overcoming hardships like job situations where even with the most positive attitude and the biggest desire for help and compassion, people did not wanted me in there.

I had a job where people made fun of me when I told them I was writing a book. They were men trying to make me change mi mine about writing positive about them, telling me about how stupid it was to write good things about men. And assured me that if I did not included sex with a touch of malice I was not going to sell it at all. One time I reacted irritated to all this and talk back to them:

"I know that the more you are trying to show your dark side trying to convince me not to write about you, the more I see the need for people in your life to love you… And honestly I don't understand why is that you have no respect for women if you came from one. Other ways you wouldn't be alive."

The morning I had the accident I called my sister who didn't answer the phone, I called Tony next. He called back minutes later to tell me he was coming to pick me up. I told the police officer that my friend was coming to help me and my son Alex... When Tony arrived he just look so young and handsome.

So the police officer asks: Is that your friend?

I said: Yes

He said: "All right" with such of excitement that made me smile.

I happen to find him attractive because he looks like my mom and one of my brothers. I feel familiar in his company. I feel taken cared of and appreciated. I believe that I am in love with his eyes.

The Man with many Wives

Recently my older sister was worried about her ex-husband being seriously ill and in danger of death. She was the first wife back then and lived in Mexico while the ex is living in USA. Her reason to worry was that if in the case that this man will die that the body will be released to the current wife or his own sister.

We were talking in the phone and it went somehow like this:

M: Why are you worried?

S: Because the is a man here in town that had many wives, he was an alcoholic and one of those days that he was drunk he fell of a high building and died…

M: Oh my God, and then?

S: Well he had many wives and some of them went to claim the body. But the people in charge won't release it until the first wife went to claim him, but guess: how many kids he made throughout his life?

M: Don't know, how many?

S: Fifty kids

M: Fifty kids! That's a lot of kids, but, don't worry, in the worst case that he may die in here, they would release the body to his Sister. Is different from Mexico. And most of it, I think he will survive this one. He is still strong. Just think positive.

S: I don't worry for me. Is just for my Daughter. We are waiting on the documents to be able to go. I just want her to catch him alive...

So far he is still alive, and this story is just an example on how men can attach people to their own existence... it sounds very irresponsible, but, who are we to judge others? Only different expressions of the divine.

The Loving Lover

That man who has had the delicacy of truth loving when it comes to lovemaking. That was able to not be aggressive with his partner, as if in the midst of its strength it hurt only coarse a signal to quit. The form of caress was soft, the way to look at you was like contemplating a beautiful landscape. He touched your hair, kissed your cheeks, forehead. He put so much attention that made you feel special. Went to your own pace, without worries, rash, nor complaints to rest. He took all the necessary time. It was as no one else exist it in the world, it was only the two of you at that magic moment.

Hands intertwined soft and had a sense of peace despite the temperature went up, was as if a sense of blessing invaded the space. A knowing that you could enjoy of true love with passion. A natural Ecstasy without the need of aphrodisiacs, a feeling of joy, of complete comfort with your body, with his body. Everything fitted perfect.

When the action finished and the rest arrived, you had the feeling of pure gratitude with life, with God, with love, the universe, everything. You felt it was worth it to live to love and be loved.

This man had shown you so much love that inspired you a deep respect. And each time that you remember you can stay there, a few moments like contemplating a beautiful landscape.

The One that makes your world Shine

This lovely, divine being... which brings you a smile when you think of him. That even if you fight him you can't be against, that one that your awareness calls to forgive, to consider, above all his sins and his failures. Because being with him is magical, it's beautiful. You can see yourself in his eyes and see love, immense love, a sweet compassion and that air of mischievous and cheerful child, that joyful spirit dancing with you, at your own pace, in your path. And that does not let you sleep, or stay stagnant in any place.

He has the power to pull out your sadness with his presence, his voice, his smell and charm. How could you stop loving, appreciating, thanking God for the joy of his existence, because your life would not be the same without him. Without his kisses, his caresses. He adds color, life and complement to your person, he makes you bigger in so many ways, he teaches you and suffers when you fall. But you know that you can rely on him to get up.

He has been your strength, it has given you the safety of trusting you, despite your failures, your mistakes, your mood swings, of hormones. He has endured everything with you and continues making your world shine, although he may be physically absent. He has been a blessing in your life and you know it. You cannot do more than feeling appreciation, joy and gratitude to the Father, the

Source, the Universe, to the God who takes care of you and always sends you Angels on Earth to take care of you and will take you back Home safe...

In this moment that I write my heart is torn by a love loss, this book has taken out so many tears that have served as therapy to heal my relationships and my life. How hard it is sometimes to forget the important people in our lives. Therefore, the songs about forget get to our soul in many occasions.

"Thank you God for suffering, because is a way of becoming more compassionate, loving, caring, understanding and humble."

THANKS TO ALL THE PEOPLE WHO INSPIRED ME TO DO THIS WORK. DEDICATED TO ALL THE MEN WHO HAVE BROKEN OUR HEART... HAVING TO FORGIVE THEM TO BE ABLE TO GO ON LIVING. I KNOW THAT THERE IS A NEED TO LOVE THEM AND THIS IS WHAT INSPIRED ME TO WRITE. WITH THE DEEPEST LOVE, I HOPE IT HAS BEEN OF YOUR SERVICE... BLESSINGS!

Thanks to my Mother:

Margarita Lopez, you are the light of my life. I owe you everything that I am. When I need to feel love is just enough with remembering your face, your smile, your voice, your good heart, your giving presence and beautiful soul.

The charm of naughty girl and loving at the same time. God has blessed you with a large family, and has you with us to show you how important, appreciated, admired and loved you are. Your food is the most delicious I've tried, no matter what restaurant I eat at... I wish I could be more like you.

I love you immensely and thank you for my life, all of your prayers and blessings, which are no doubt being attended and heard in heaven. Thank you Mama.

María Ortíz